You Are My Sunshine
The Story of a Remarkable Old Dog

By Sandy Kamen Wisniewski

Edited and designed by Simone Ogloza

You Are My Sunshine
A Product of SKW Publishing
A division of SKW Enterprises

For information address You Are My Sunshine c/o AEAR, P.O. Box 7343,
Libertyville, IL 60048.
www.aear.org

Book edited and designed by Simone Ogloza

ISBN-13: 978-1539661009

ISBN-10: 1539661008

Many thanks to Simone Ogloza for proofreading and designing this book. Also, thank you to my husband, Chuck Wisniewski, for reviewing the book as well.

In loving memory of Bear.

Introduction

Thank you for purchasing this book. I am proud to say that every purchase of this book is going to help the animals at Animal Education and Rescue. Within this little book's pages, you will read about one of the greatest loves of my life: my dog Bear. Please understand that it was written with great thought for a higher purpose other than just therapy for me. In it, I hope to bring you an honest story filled with lessons I have learned from a very special dog that entered my life for a very short time.

Because it is written with my truth, you will notice references to "the universe," "angels," "spirit guides" and more of what might be referred to as "metaphysical beliefs." If that belief system doesn't serve you, I hope you can take those words and maybe consider replacing them with "God" or "subconscious" or whatever feels right to you. We may not share the same beliefs of the same "higher power(s)," BUT love IS something I think we can all agree on. Love is ultimately the most important and most powerful tool we have available to us. Love binds us, gives us a sense of purpose, is all wise and connects us in the best possible way.

Always in love,
Sandy Kamen Wisniewski

-One-

My spirit couldn't let her go. I didn't know how. Knowing I was being selfish, I couldn't help it. I said out loud to her, "Please don't go yet."

Then I heard Bear talking to me. We all receive those inner voices that "talk" to us, it's just a matter of learning to listen. Those messages are not delivered in words, per se, but in a kind of "knowing" or silent internal voice. Bear said, "Write my story. Tell others about me and about our love and then maybe you can let me go." But I wasn't so sure…

****

Making a left onto the drive at animal control, I navigated through the chain link gates that were propped open and parked my car. Getting out of the car, I was not at all aware that my life was about to change and grow in a way I never could have guessed. I was about to meet what would turn out to be one of the greatest loves of my life.

With each hardship, each curve ball and my share of tragic

happenings, I have had an opportunity to learn. More often than not, I didn't like the challenges, sometimes even gritted my teeth and moaned, thinking, *why me, why me?* Yet little did I know that another series of lessons was on its way to me on one warm, sunny, spring day in 2013 when I drove home with a hairy, old dog stinking up my car.

As the founder and director of Animal Education and Rescue, I wear many hats for my grassroots, non-profit humane society that I started in 2003. One of those hats is Intake Coordinator. That means I choose which animals to rescue. Once I make the choice to take the animal, there is much more to do until he gets adopted.

First, I evaluate the dog then choose what home he will live in until he gets adopted (or I personally foster him if there isn't a home available, which happens a lot). I arrange for medical care or communicate with the foster family about medical care. If I'm fostering the animal, I deal with behavior issues. If the dog goes to a foster home, I regularly communicate with them and assist them with medical or behavior issues that arise. We take animals from people who no longer want them, stray animals and animals from local animal control facilities.

On that particular spring day that I entered animal control, Susan, the senior animal warden, a rough-around-the-edges woman who wears her heart on her sleeve, was sitting behind her desk. She got right to it. "Oh, I'm glad you are here. There is this dog here. The story is so sad. You are not going to believe it..."

"What?" I cringed, preparing myself to hear another heart-wrenching story.

"The man who owned her went to jail and the girlfriend to a mental hospital. You can imagine it wasn't good. They had a dog that's here now. She's fourteen, Sandy, it's tragic. She's sitting on the cold, cement floor and who is going to take her?"

Susan was smart. She slathered on the sorrow, playing into my soft heart. What she shares is always the truth, but is told in a dramatic way that works well. I would do the same thing if I were in her shoes. She's in a rough spot at a big, city-run animal control facility. She did what she had to do to save the animals that came to her. We both knew her game and we both agreed to play it. She also knew I was a sucker for real hard-luck cases.

After a long pause, I conceded. "Okay, I'll take a look...but *only* a look," I stressed.

"You can go back," she said.

I opened the steel door in the office that leads to the rows of kennels. The creak of the door caused the dogs in their dog runs to irrupt into a nearly deafening barking frenzy. I made my way down the aisle, both sides lined with dog runs, looking from my left to my right. Variations of pit bulls danced and jumped about in different states of total excitement and utter chaos.

About three quarters of the way down the aisle on the left, I saw her. She was sitting in the center of her chain link enclosure. She was a black and tan, stocky-built shepherd mix. Her hair was coming out in tufts and she had two unsightly, large skin tags dangling from her right front leg near the elbow. She looked right at me, seemingly oblivious to the ruckus of the dogs all around her, smiling widely. All resolve I had to NOT take her crumbled instantaneously.

"Hi, baby," I said, leaning forward and looking through the chain link kennel door to where she sat quietly, "you wanna get outta here?" She looked up at me with deep, brown, soulful eyes and smiled wider. "I'll be right back," I assured her.

I walked quickly back to the office door. I let the door to the kennel slam behind me as I entered the office. It was blissfully quieter, at least in comparison to the jarring commotion on the other side. Susan was sitting at her desk. "So?" she asked, "isn't that sad?"

"Okay, I can take her just to get her out of this place. I'll put her in my office. But keep looking for a rescue to take her. At fourteen, I know she probably won't get adopted. If she's lucky, she'll have six months. But she can't have any more time here. She deserves more."

After completing the paperwork, Susan brought the dog up to the office and handed me the leash. "Her name is Bear and she knows it."

-Two-

Life for me is a juggling act of dozens of daily activities within more daily tasks and wrapped up with hundreds of interactions with people and animals throughout each day. Absolutely nothing is predictable and I often refer to my life's work, especially with Animal Education and Rescue, like living in the center of a person's brain with Bipolar Disorder. The ups and downs of AEAR are like a roller coaster ride. I have come to accept AEAR as it is and learned to manage the unpredictability of it. In general, I have to say, I like *most* of what I do.

While I realize my lifestyle is not the norm and most people (I would venture to guess) think I'm a little off kilter, maybe eccentric even, I have learned over time to stop trying to fit into a box and just do my best to live an authentic life as an evolving person. But staying balanced within the chaos…well, now, THAT'S the ultimate challenge. Thankfully, my company Mindful Spirit, centered in meditation, natural healing and health, is the soothing balm I need to keep the rocky boat of my life from tipping over.

****

Bear initially settled into my office, but I soon realized that she was so passive and easy-going, I could probably easily integrate her with my crew of behaviorally challenged, misfit dogs at what I fondly call "the orphanage" (my house). One by one, I introduced her to the dogs. As I suspected, she settled in as if she had always been there, the other dogs completely unaffected by her entrance into the pack.

Watching the dogs outside as they romp, sniff, explore and create ruckus in the backyard, the energy level they share at a high decibel, the stark contrast between their collective energy and Bear's energy was obvious.

Foster dog Lucy is a six-year-old, black as midnight Shar Pei and Lab mix. She came into my care two years ago after I received a call from animal control about a "very scared dog at the kennel that had scars all over and recently must have given birth." (Her puppies were never found.) They said that she would not do well at the local shelter and asked me if we would be able to take her.

With pockmark scars on her front legs, face and neck, we suspect Lucy may have been used for dog fighting. She has a huge L-shaped scar on her neck, deeper than I have ever seen, made by some gruesome injury only she knows about.

Lucy believes it's her job to protect our property. She is always on high alert, monitoring the fence lines and leaping on and off the picnic table looking for danger. She soars onto and over our shorter, interior fences with ease, looking for little critters in parts of the back yard we have wanted to be dog free, which clearly aren't off limits to her, as far as Lucy is concerned.

Her scar's scab has healed long ago and her milk has, of course, dried up, but her emotional scars remain. When we have any adults over to our house, Lucy darts around them, keeping a wide berth, near hysterical, whining and acting like a wild dog might act. Ironically, she is the exact opposite with people under about fifteen years old. She loves kids and even feels a sense of comfort when she is with them. She has grown to love us on her terms and with a stubborn streak that drives me crazy sometimes.

Also at the orphanage is Magoo, or Goo, as his many Facebook admirers and AEAR volunteers know him. He's a fourteen-pound, senior Poodle mix who was found dumped on the streets of suburban Lake County and picked up by animal control. Blind and mostly deaf, animal control reached out to me as a last-ditch effort to save the dog's life. Little did I know that Goo suffers with severe separation anxiety. It's impossible to know whether it came on due to his blindness or if he was always that way. I believe it's likely the latter since I have had other blind dogs that weren't nearly that anxious.

When I am not holding Goo, he is frantically searching for me, barking incessantly. It is, in all honestly, nearly maddening. Outside, when I put him down to go potty, he's quiet just long enough to lift his leg then he's off on a quest of loud barking, calling for me. Until I pick him up, he walks around bumping into objects and dogs like a hairy, black, pinball game's silver ball.

Since I took him in, about three years ago, I have had a few different dog pouches I have worn so that I can be hands-free while carrying him. The first one I had was a sling style that I wore like a carrier bag with Goo at my hip. It was a miracle and Goo would settle in the pouch like a baby being swaddled.

After carrying him around like that for many months, I found myself at the chiropractor weekly with terrible neck issues. I had no idea what was causing my neck pain. But while lying on the doctor's table waiting for her to come into the room, it dawned on me. That darn pouch was causing the pain!

So I switched to a front pouch. The equal pressure on both of my shoulders and my back was better by far than the sling style pouch, but over time the front pouch caused my upper back to hurt. So now I limit using the front pouch to short periods of time to ease back pain and when I am not using it, I either do everything one-handed with Goo in the other arm or just do my best to try and tune out the non-stop, hysterical barking.

People often say to me, "poor Goo, it must be so hard for him." My response is always, "I don't know about that. I'd say, poor Sandy," and laugh. Then I add, "but I am committed for the long haul."

Then there's Mouse, a Miniature Pinscher and Chihuahua mix. She came to stay with us about a year ago. She has what looks like a form of cerebral palsy. She stumbles as she walks, her legs buckling in contorted ways. Whenever she stops moving, more often than not, her legs splay into the splits which looks terribly painful but clearly is not, judging by the alert and adventurous look on her face. I am sometimes juggling Mouse and Goo or carrying them both at once.

We are excited that Mouse was recently fitted with a little pink cart: a two-wheeled device that allows her to use her fully functioning front legs to carry her back legs with the assistance of the back wheels. Because of the way her back legs get strapped in at the rear end of the cart, above the wheels, she can move her back legs in a way that is actually providing her therapy that may strengthen her legs. It's been delightful watching her buzz around in her cart.

Star, another long-term foster dog, was discarded in a wooded area of an impoverished town, well-known for its gang activity and drug dealers. Star was set free, along with her three littermates, at eight-weeks-old. Periodically observed by residents, no one bothered to contact the authorities all winter long. How they survived is unknown. In the spring, the wild pack of then-adolescent canines was harder to ignore. Finally, someone alerted the authorities who then contacted Cindy, a friend of mine who is a licensed humane investigator. For weeks, Cindy tried to catch the puppies to no avail, finally setting humane traps to catch them.

The last puppy to be caught was Star; her dead brother was lying near her. She never left his side. We learned later that the brother died of parvovirus: a contagious, terribly painful stomach virus. The two female littermates, caught the week before her, died of parvovirus at an animal shelter just a few days later.

By some miracle, Star was spared from parvovirus, but the scarring of her life in the woods and watching her brother suffer left her with life-long consistent, persistent anxiety. At ten-years-old, Star is still wound super tight and distrusts all humans except for me.

Those are some of the long-term animals that live with my family. My husband, Chuck, and I regularly welcome other animals into the orphanage until they find foster homes or permanent homes. We rehabilitate them by showing them love and consistency, as well as provide whatever medical attention they need. Finally, we celebrate the day each animal moves on to a better life with a new, loving family.

-Three-

Bear arrived in my care, thankfully, already spayed. But because of her age, I opted not to remove a large fatty tumor on her side, situated under her arm. If she lived long enough for it to bother her, the doctor and I agreed to address it again then. She also had some unsightly, large skin tags on her elbows, which were not painful and she could easily live with.

A few weeks went by and Susan still wasn't able to find another rescue group to take the fourteen-year-old dog. Meanwhile, I was going about my hectic, fast-paced daily life, juggling my businesses, taking care of the ever-changing number of foster animals in my care, as well as my daily tasks as mom, wife and house manager. But it was not lost to me, even amongst the swirling buzz of a busy life, the bond I was beginning to feel for the old shepherd mix. I had fostered literally thousands of animals in the eleven years running Animal Education and Rescue. But this old girl…there was something special about her. She was growing on me, or shall I say, in my heart.

Three weeks after Bear's arrival, on a sunny summer

afternoon, I was in my car getting ready to leave the animal hospital's parking lot when I heard my cell phone beep that I had a text message. I looked at the phone and saw that it was from Susan: "Bear's owner came in to check on her. She got out of the hospital. Wanted to make sure she was ok. She said Bear's 10."

"Whoopee!" I yelled out loud. The difference between fourteen and ten for a dog is huge. She could have some life left with someone who could love her. *She has time to begin again*, I thought to myself. The following day, I called the animal hospital and scheduled surgery to have Bear's lump and skin tags removed.

My next goal with Bear was to start her on an exercise regimen to help her take off a few extra pounds. Lisa, an AEAR volunteer, offered to come over a few times a week to walk Bear. I took up the task of walking her on alternate days. I also made sure to measure out the correct amount of food at each meal for a dog her size. I take physical health seriously and know good health can prolong life.

On her daily walks, Bear moved quite slowly and lumbered along. We meandered at a pace that nearly put me to sleep. After a few short weeks, Bear would abruptly stop walking before we even left the driveway of the house. I tried coaxing her and baby-talking her to no avail. I didn't have time to keep trying to get her to walk, so we headed back inside. The next day, Lisa had the same results. After a few days of this behavior, we realized that Bear had caught on to all that exercise nonsense and wasn't up to the program. So that ended her formal exercise regime.

Every day, everywhere I went in the house—everywhere I sat, everywhere I stood—Bear was right there. Chuck began calling Bear my "shadow." When I left the house and returned, she was right at whatever door I left through, looking at the door and waiting for me. Her loyalty was nearly immediate, which surprised me and made my fondness for her grow even more.

****

The mission of Animal Education and Rescue is to bring people and animals together through education, therapy and rescue. I speak regularly at schools, teaching kids about responsible pet ownership, how to approach a dog, bite prevention and much more. The audience dictates what animals I bring. After Bear recovered from her surgery, she began joining me at speaking engagements.

One morning I was standing in front of about twenty, five-and-six-year-old squirmy, giggly, excited kids in the empty lunchroom of a local public school. I asked the kids to sit on the floor in a circle where I would lead each animal I brought with me around the circle for the kids to meet and pet. I started with a ferret, then a rabbit and so on. Bear sat waiting patiently with a volunteer outside the circle. This was her first public appearance. When it was Bear's turn, I said to her, "Bear, please go around the circle and say hello to each child."

Bear stood up and looked towards me. I went over to her and took the leash from the volunteer and said, "Go on now, Bear." I pointed towards a child, "go say hello." The leash loosely in my hand, Bear walked over to a child and waited for the child to pet her. The little boy with blond hair smiled widely and gently petted Bear on her head. She leaned into the hand and nearly closed her eyes, her mouth open in a smile. After a few seconds, Bear opened her eyes, perked up her ears and moved over to the next child and received some attention. In a few minutes she had flawlessly completed visiting each child in the whole circle. All the kids were giggling and sighing with delight, watching Bear as she went about her work. I was totally surprised. They were clearly impressed.

Thus began Bear's regal career as a volunteer with Animal Education and Rescue. She came to pet therapy at the nursing home, presentations for scout troops, our new volunteer meetings and much more. She was simply amazing every time she joined me at one of our programs. It was as if she was molded specifically to show people love and compassion in a gentle, calm way.

Throughout the months that followed, I embraced her positive energy even more. At times of stress or worry, all I needed to do was look into Bear's face and was reminded that all was right in the world. As Bobby McFerrin sang, I was sure Bear would sing the same words if she could, "Don't worry, be happy."

-Four-

Due to some unforeseen issues, after about three months in my care, Bear moved to another foster home. The calm, tranquil music Bear brought to my chaotic life vanished in thin air when I dropped her off at the new foster home. A few weeks after Bear left, as soon as I was able, I brought her back home. On the drive back to the house, I looked over at her sitting there contently and was surprised by my thought... *now I am whole again.* Of all the hundreds of dogs I have fostered and the dozens of dogs I have owned, I had not felt such a soul-to-soul connection with any of them. It felt like we had been soul mates before.

Bear lived with me for a year and not a single application came in for her. It was what I anticipated. People just typically don't adopt old dogs. The most common things I hear when discussing adopting an older pet with people is, "I don't want the dog to die so soon. It would break my heart." Or, "I just lost a dog and it was terrible. I don't want to go through a dog dying so soon again."

"Chuck, I'm thinking about adopting Bear," I said, as we

sipped on our morning coffee. It was a bitter cold day and looking over at Bear I couldn't have felt warmer. Chuck basically supported whatever I wanted so he said, "okay." I knew it was ultimately my decision. For me, it wasn't the fact that she was old and that I wouldn't have her long that made me hesitate. Having her in my care made me appreciate her age. She was calm, wise and easy to care for. But I was concerned about her needing more medical care sooner, which could be costly.

Setting that concern aside, I decided she needed me and I needed her for as long as we had together. As an adopted person myself, I believe very strongly that everyone needs to belong to someone. Whether Bear consciously knew it or not, I wanted her to have a real family, not a just foster family.

My decision was spurred on more quickly because we had a very special event coming up where we invited people who adopted animals from us to be part of an adoption party and reunion. During that event, I formally adopted Bear. Bear had a family and I had my girl. I couldn't have been more proud or felt more whole than the day I wrapped my arms around my new fur-daughter and knew we were really, genuinely family.

Adopting her made everything with Bear seem more real to me—more permanent and yet, ironically, so temporary too. At eleven-years-old, we didn't have much time left together. That fact came forward to my conscious mind in a daily mantra, reminding me to try and live in as many small moments with Bear as possible. Ironically, that attitude of living life in the moment spilled out into other aspects of my life as well. I found myself stopping periodically during the day and just appreciating those moments more deeply.

When Bear was roughly twelve, she began needing help getting in and out of the car for her various activities with AEAR. She slowly made her way to the car and, when I opened the door, I could sense her contemplating how she would get in. Methodically, she lifted one front leg up and waited while I gently wrapped my arms around her lower belly and hoisted her inside. Once settled on the seat comfortably, she looked at me with gratitude. As we drove along, she sat comfortably and expectantly, gazing at the scenery, waiting calmly for what was to come, knowing whatever it was, it was going to be done together. The difference was that an obvious tiredness was washing over her.

She was eating, drinking, pooping and peeing normally, so I wasn't alarmed that she may be sick. But occasionally I would look at her and silently brace myself. In my life I had already owned many dogs, walking through all the cycles and seasons of their lives together, to know Bear and I were entering the final stage of her life.

This past June, Bear and I were at the nursing home with volunteers and other animals. As usual, one of the youth volunteers was taking Bear around. Fifteen minutes into the one-hour program, Nicole, the youth club girl who was holding Bear, came over to me. "Sandy, Bear won't move. I tried pulling her and she just sits there. Lauren is holding her leash so I could come and get you."

Following Nicole down the hallway, I saw Bear was sitting down with Lauren standing beside her. I took the leash from Lauren. I tried coaxing Bear by gently pulling her leash. "Bear, come on sweetie, let's go." She seemed to be ignoring me. I thought maybe she was being stubborn, so I said more sternly, "Bear, come on now, we can't just sit here, let's go!" She looked at me and then down the hallway with tired, spent eyes. She hung her head low, her shoulders rounded. It was in that instant that I knew she was done with pet therapy for good.

Finally, I was able to convince her we weren't going to continue and instead were going home. So she reluctantly got up and followed me back towards the front doors. We waited for the other volunteers to finish up and meet up with us. I forced on a smile and thanked everyone for coming that night.

As Bear and I walked out of the front doors of the building together, I could feel the curtains close behind us…that show was over.

-Five-

Meditation with Dogs is one of our unique events, which combines dog therapy and the calming qualities of meditation. A local grooming shop lets us hold the meditations at her place on Sundays twice a month. I invite people to join me, with or without a dog. I bring with me anywhere from three to six older dogs. During these special mornings, I lead the group through a guided meditation, followed by a discussion on spiritual growth. The dogs wander from person to person until they decide where they will eventually lie down. Bear was one of the crew and, after going from person to person saying hello, she always hunkered down beside me on the floor.

In addition to the meditation sessions, Bear still accompanied me to our monthly new volunteer orientations. On those evenings, when people trickled in, she meandered over to them, looked up at their faces, a wide grin on her face, and waited to be petted. As Bear connected with each person, you could feel the positive, calming energy exchange between them.

Once everyone settled into their seats, I'd ask, "Has Bear said hello to everyone? If she hasn't please raise your hand." Sometimes people slipped in a few minutes late or a cluster of people came in all at once, so it wasn't uncommon for Bear to have missed a person or two. If anyone raised his or her hand, I said to Bear, "Now, Bear, go on over there and say hello." Happy to oblige, she slowly rose and plodded over to the person she hadn't greeted.

A few months ago, I noticed Bear was slowing down even more. She no longer got up to greet people at the new volunteer orientation and mostly slept through the entire meeting. That was a significant change for her. Additionally, at home, it took her great effort to follow me around the house. I noticed sometimes Bear had a far off look on her face. It often seemed as if she was looking somewhere else entirely, a bit curious and with a kind of peaceful resignation. Could it possibly be that I was actually seeing her looking towards the other side? *Not possible,* I told myself. *It's my overactive imagination.*

Then one day Bear woke up with an upset tummy and she had diarrhea outside. That was new for Bear, so I took notice right away. I fed her a bland dinner and there was a slight improvement. But in my gut I could feel my own stomach churning uncomfortably…something just didn't feel right.

The following weekend, I was scheduled to take a certification class on Reiki for Dogs. Reiki is a form of energy healing. I am a Reiki practitioner and Spiritual Energy Healer for people. Through my other company, Mindful Spirit, I provide one-on-one spiritual healing sessions for clients, as well as various classes and group-guided meditations. I signed up for the Reiki for Dogs class, interested in learning new methods specifically with animals and techniques to refine my different skills. The woman that was teaching the class was a well-known and respected holistic veterinarian and Reiki Master.

The first day of class, I arrived a bit early, smiled at the few people already there and found a seat. The doctor hurried in shortly after I arrived. Frazzled, she mumbled to no one in particular that she wasn't a morning person. She wore her graying, shoulder length hair in a braid at the side of her head and was wearing flowing and comfortable clothes. I found myself smiling at her as I watched her get ready. She was as real as one gets, without any facades or layers and I immediately liked her.

We were told in advance that there weren't going to be any dogs the first day of class, but that they would bring dogs in for us to work on the next day. Midway through the day, the doctor mentioned that the dogs she usually had come to her classes were unavailable the following day. She said she was scrambling to find dogs that would be appropriate. "Don't worry," she assured us. "I'll get some for you to work with." But I could tell she was worried.

At break time, I approached her and said, "I run a humane society for animals. I have a wide variety of pet therapy dogs. I am more than happy to bring you as many dogs as you need."

She smiled widely and sighed with relief, "That would be great. Really, thanks."

That night, I thought about who I would bring. Energy healing work is, if nothing else, relaxing. But it can also do much more. There are seven energy fields on the body called chakras. If any one of those energy fields is muddy or blocked, it can cause physical and emotional issues. By clearing them,—gently placing your hands on or near the body's energy fields—physical, spiritual and emotional pain can dissipate.

The following morning, I loaded Spike, a 14-year-old Miniature Pincher, Petey, a senior Chihuahua and Bear into the car and we headed over to class. We arrived a bit early. The doctor's assistant showed us to an area they had set up for us where there were tarps covering the carpeting. The first half of the day, the dogs just relaxed with us as the doctor prepared us for the afternoon's hands-on energy work.

In the afternoon, two more dogs arrived and we divided into groups of two or three people per dog. The three dogs I brought were way more concerned with where I was than being with the people they were assigned to spend the hour with. Because all three dogs kept trying to be nearest to me, we all sat very close to each other.

Our teacher walked around the room, overseeing our hand positions on the dogs. I had Petey with me and Bear was just a few feet from me, with two women around her. She sat facing me, her eyes on me at all times. Her mouth was open and her eyes at half-mast. She was content sitting with the ladies, especially knowing I was just an arms-length away. The room was quiet except for the occasional gentle, soothing whispers of encouraging words people were giving the dogs.

Looking around the room, an overwhelming sadness washed over me. At first I didn't know why I felt that way, at least until instinctively I turned my attention to Bear. As I looked at Bear, her eyes partially on me and partially in some far off place, that feeling I had of Bear pulling away from me the past two weeks was stronger than ever. My memory of that time was that I swallowed down tears and worried about Bear, feeling like our time together was slipping away.

After the hands-on healing, we took a break. During the break, Bear proceeded to have diarrhea on the carpet before I could get her outside. I felt terrible about it, but everyone was more than kind and helped me clean it up. *This stomach issue needs to be addressed again, this time more seriously*, I thought to myself.

The doctor came up to me after clean up and said, "I have holistic medication that I can give you to give Bear. It will hopefully help her stomach. I have a few pills here today and I'll send you the rest in the mail." *What a loving gesture*, I thought and gratefully accepted. She brought me one of the pills and I promptly put it in Bear's mouth, forcing her to swallow it. "Please, baby, get well, please," I whispered in her ear. "I can't lose you yet."

****

The following week, I thought back many times about what I had learned at the Reiki for Dogs class and was so grateful to the doctor and her staff for all they taught me. I already knew that the soul of an animal is no different than that of a human being. But what was reinforced to me was that the big difference between humans and other animals is that animals don't overthink things. They don't wear their egos on their shoulders. They are who they are and don't apologize for it. Also, I have asked myself more than once why I didn't try to do more healing with Bear than I did. While I did practice some healing for her, I think I knew her time was drawing near and instinctually and subconsciously knew there was nothing I could do about it.

The medication for Bear's tummy didn't seem to be working, so a trip to her conventional, medical veterinarian was in order. It was a warm, sunny day in August. I made the appointment for noon and didn't think much of it the morning of the appointment and just went about normal business. Fifteen minutes before our appointment, I loaded Bear into the car and we headed out to see the doctor. Looking back, I am so, so grateful that I didn't know what was going to happen.

At the veterinarian's office, Bear saw Dr. Williamson. He examined her and couldn't find anything particularly wrong. I gave a staff member a stool sample so they could test it for parasites. We decided to be conservative and give her medication and see if the medicine cleared up the diarrhea.

As I was leaving with Bear, I felt all my worries wash away, relieved that my suspicions about the coming days were wrong. *We have a day, a week, maybe a year,* I thought, as we walked to the car together. We were almost at the car when Bear abruptly stopped and retched and retched, trying to throw up but nothing came out. *That's new*, I thought, that familiar dread instantaneously filling me up again. I turned her around and went back inside. The doctor happened to still be in the small waiting area. "Bear just threw up," I said, "well, nothing came up, though." He bent down and felt around her belly.

"Feel this," he said.

I reached underneath her and pressed on her abdomen. It was hard, bloated and round. "Oh, no," I sighed, feeling my heart drop to my knees. "Bloat."

"Yes, I suspect that might be it. I am surprised because on examination she seemed okay. It must have just happened now. We can run a few tests to determine if it is bloat for sure."

Bloat is when the stomach flips or partially flips over and cuts off the two ends that lead into the stomach. Gasses fill up inside the stomach and cause the stomach to bloat out. Without emergency surgery, the dog dies. However, the surgery is costly and nothing is guaranteed.

The doctor came back into the waiting room after completing a few tests. It was bloat.

The cost for surgery would be $3,000-$4,000. Bear was twelve-years-old. The doctor suspected the diarrhea was likely part of an underlying medical issue. The x-ray showed a suspected tumor that would be inoperable. A decision needed to be made quickly before Bear began to suffer from the painful symptoms of bloat.

It was time to let her go.

Of all the animals I have had to say goodbye to, the scale of pain I was in for my beloved Bear could not be matched. As I sat on the floor of the exam room with her one last time, I whispered into her ear, "I love you, Sunshine. I'll see you again." And in my subconscious I said, *wait for me.* The subconscious is a tricky thing. While we think it can't be heard, it certainly can.

Leaving the animal hospital without Bear, a heavy haze surrounded me. The world grew suddenly small, mute and gray as if I was being sucked into a dark, colorless box. I drove home on autopilot, tears streaming freely down my face, fully present in the wretched, unwanted pain. In a whisper, I sang the song I often whispered in Bear's ear: "you are my sunshine, my only sunshine…"

-Six-

On most days I walk many miles. Walking is my therapy: my way of centering and connecting with the energies constantly expressing themselves in nature and in the universe, those seen and unseen to the human eye. During my walks is when I, more often than any other time, communicate with my guides and angels.

In this past year, I have also studied mediumship: communicating with souls who have passed on. With the teaching and guidance of spiritual leaders, I practice daily exercises to hone in on my psychic abilities. (Everyone has metaphysical abilities; it's a matter of learning to practice expanding them.)

The day Bear died, I decided it was time to put all my training to the test. I was determined to connect with Bear. I was determined to *see* Bear again.

That afternoon as I walked and cried, I felt like a heavy weight was sitting on my chest and breathing was hard. It was also as if part of me left my body. I'd look down at myself as I walked, puzzled as to how my chest could really feel so heavy when I didn't see anything heavy on it. And I was perplexed further as I walked because I could see my arms and legs pumping away even though I was essentially numb.

My shoes felt miles of pavement and Bear never came to me.

The following morning, I set off again walking, determined to connect with Bear. I decided to walk to my office for my company Mindful Spirit. I rent space in a well-known chiropractor's office, about three miles away. I was going to drop off a flyer I designed to display on the front counter.

No more than five minutes into my walk, my daughter, Sarah, called me on my cell phone. She explained that one of her friends was having serious emotional issues. We discussed her friend's dilemma at length, brainstorming how we could best help her. By the time I was done with my call, I was almost at my destination. That only gave me enough time to do some energy healing on myself. I visualized my hands, one by one, moving to each of my seven chakras, giving myself loving, healing energy from the universe.

Arriving at the office, the women who worked there were all up front behind the big reception desk. It was near lunchtime and the office was closed for patients. As I was placing the flyers for my next class on the front desk, the office manager said, "I've been meaning to talk to you. I wanted to get back to you about your question..." As we were talked, the conversation became a bit more chit-chatty and some of the other ladies gathered around to join the conversation.

Gayle, one of the massage therapists said to me, "You know the drum you were using last week at your meditation? I'm still hearing that drum," she said, blinking back tears.

Perplexed by her strong reaction to the drum I said, "Is that good or bad?"

"It's good," she smiled, "but I am not sure why I am still hearing it."

"The drum is a very powerful instrument for bringing insight to people. Native Americans believe very strongly in it. Shamans use them all the time. I love using it, especially when I guide people to find their animal protector or on a guided journey of some kind."

By now, all six women had shifted their attention to our conversation and were gathered around closer as they casually munched on their lunches. "That's so interesting," Agnes, a pretty, blonde woman said. "What's your animal protector spirit, Sandy?"

"It's a bear," I said, subconsciously touching the bear pendant necklace I received for my birthday last year. I wear it every day and haven't taken it off. I went on to explain what the bear symbol means as they listened intently. Happy to share my knowledge about animal protectors, I didn't put two-and-two together that of any conversations we could have, I was talking about my animal protector, the "bear." Plus, I happened to come on a Thursday, the only day that the doctor wasn't there and the only day that would have allowed us any time for conversation of any length…and I just so happened to come exactly at their lunchtime.

After nearly an hour of conversation, we finished up and I put my ear buds into my ears, turned the music on my phone, slung my backpack across my shoulders and headed out. Once more my attention went to the task at hand: to receive a message from Bear.

I have two cell phones. My phone with the pink case around it is for Mindful Spirit. I hardly ever get calls on it. It just so happened it was in the pocket of my jeans that afternoon, whereas typically it's in my backpack. As I walked along, concentrating on my breathing, I felt a vibration next to my thigh. Feeling the spot, I noticed it was my pink phone and I pulled it out. I looked at the screen. There was a message waiting for me in my voice mail.

Taking my ear buds out of my ears, I listened to the message as I walked along. It was a woman calling, saying she had some questions for me. She sounded apprehensive and slightly embarrassed and left her phone number. I called back right away.

"Hi Elaine, this is Sandy from Mindful Spirit."

"Hi Sandy. I met you at one of your classes. It was Finding Your Animal Protector."

"Oh, okay," I said, "the one over the summer at the forest preserve?"

"Yes, that one. I was very impressed by it. I feel kind of silly asking this, but I felt compelled to call you..." she paused and cleared her throat. "My parents had a dog...it wasn't really my dog because I haven't lived with my parents for a long time. And the dog just," she stopped talking and cleared her throat again, "died. You see I wasn't even home, I mean my home or theirs when the dog died. I was on vacation. When they called me, it hit me really hard. I mean *really* hard..."

Walking along a sidewalk near a park, I listened to this woman and felt this kind of zoning in feeling, like squinting one eye and looking through a telescope with the other eye. "I know exactly how you feel," I responded. Then I added, "I just lost my dog suddenly. She was very important to me."

"Oh, wow. That's so weird. My parents' dog died yesterday."

"My dog died yesterday, too," I told her, my words not missing the irony of the conversation. I added, "Losing a dog is one of the hardest things a dog lover can go through. Most people don't understand the pain you feel when you lose your dog."

"I know, but this wasn't really my dog..."

"But it felt like he was, right?"

"Yea, I guess he did. It's so final. It's such a strange thing to do...put a dog to sleep."

"I know. I agree. I am so sorry for your loss, Elaine. Allow yourself to grieve. You are entitled to your feelings. It would not be unusual for you to go through all the five stages of grief that you would if a person died." Stepping off a curb and onto a side street I added, "I know I've got a long way to go."

I listened to her share her feelings some more and the conversation was wrapping up.

"You've really helped me. I'm so glad I called. It's really weird that I called you, I think, but I guess it was meant to be."

"Yes, Elaine, it was," I agreed, nodding my head. "If you need me, I am a phone call away." We hung up and a wave of deep, intense gratitude came over me. I couldn't deny that Bear was with me, guiding me.

By the end of the walk, I had retraced the past few hours and realized that Bear had been trying to reach me at the chiropractor's office, but I wasn't listening, so she did something drastic and obvious by bringing Elaine and me together.

Chuckling to myself I thought, *she knows I am good at giving advice, but not always as good at following the advice I give others.* Further, she reminded me that I am needed and have a purpose here and need to keep focusing on not only taking care of myself but also taking care of others.

-Seven-

The following day, I headed outside for a long walk. This time I took a new route on the east side of town that led to a forest preserve trail. On either side of the trail, there are big, old trees, shrubs and brush. Due to some recent rains, water flooded the floor of either side of the trail, giving the area a majestic landscape. The weather was warm and a bit muggy. The sun blazed down onto the trees, their limbs and leaves creating sparkling shimmering golden color as I walked the gravel path.

It was during that walk that Bear came to me again, but this time I saw her in my mind's eye, or third eye as it's often referred. She was sitting in a darkened space between what appeared to be this world and the other side. It was very dim where she sat, a cave-like place. Behind her, there was an opening where I could see a bright white light. It didn't hurt my eyes at all. Suddenly Echo appeared at the mouth of the opening from the light. This was not the first time I had seen Echo since his passing.

Many years ago, a young woman called the office asking me if we could take her dog. She explained that the ten-year-old

Border collie mix lived at the pet food testing facility from birth until nine-years-old. The facility was closing down for good and the staff that worked at the testing facility was trying to find homes for the 300 dogs and cats living there. The woman heard about what was happening and agreed to take a Border collie mix. She named him Echo.

She went on to say that she had Echo for a year and he never adjusted at all. She said he was completely shut down and that he never went to the bathroom outside. She laid down pee pads everywhere and he went to the bathroom when she wasn't around. Echo was constantly terrified. She was moving and couldn't take him with her. She said, "It's hard to explain, but believe me I have tried everything."

Thinking she hadn't tried everything, I agreed to take him. I knew I had more experience than most when it came to dogs and I could fix him. After many years of having Echo, I had to admit that I, too, was out of options for him. Ultimately, I just accepted Echo for who he was and celebrated any tiny improvement I saw during the three-plus years he was with me. It was an extremely difficult time for me, having Echo. (His full story is for another day and time and someday I will tell it in its entirety.)

The day I said goodbye to Echo, he had no quality of life left.

It was really one of the hardest goodbyes ever because I felt such a deep sense of responsibility for him. Over the years, Echo had grown to love me in his own autistic, Echo kind of way. When we parted, I was so worried who would take care of him on the other side.

More than a year later, Scrappy, one of my own dogs, developed a tumor on his face. It was inoperable. We kept him comfortable until it was time to say goodbye. The afternoon after we put Scrappy to sleep, I went on a walk. As I walked, I tried to soothe my aching heart, breathing deeply and just trying to relax. That's when a vision came to me.

In the vision, I could sense Scrappy's soul near me. I couldn't see him in his Earthly form, but felt his energy out in front of me as I walked. Then suddenly I saw Echo come through what appeared as an opening where there was a white light. He stood before me, in my mind's eye, his head held high, tail up and over his back and chest out. Confidence poured out from him. My breath caught.

It was then that I saw Echo look towards the energy that I knew was Scrappy. I knew that Echo was calling for Scrappy, he was welcoming him to the other side. I was completely floored. My insecure Echo, afraid, really terrified in this world, was now leading others not only into the other side, but I knew he was a leader in general. I was so proud.

So the day I walked on that trail viewing that scene, tears rolled down my cheeks, Bear was in this dark cave-like place of what was clearly the "in between," looking towards me as if I was on television. She was loyally waiting for my instructions. Echo stood in silhouette by the light, lovingly and gently, mentally calling to Bear to come. Bear looked at Echo, then looked back at me. My spirit couldn't let her go. I didn't know how. I knew I was being selfish, but I couldn't help it and said out loud to her, "Please don't go yet."

Mentally, Bear spoke to me heart-to-heart. She said, "Write my story. Tell others about me and about our love and then maybe you can let me go. I will be with you until then." Selfish as I felt, I also knew we had a game plan.

****

The following evening, Chuck and I headed out to Highland Park, a town twenty-five minutes away, to work and attend a fundraising gala for Infinity Foundation, a non-profit holistic education center. I was among the forty or so practitioners assigned a table and offering a free ten-minute service. I chose to demonstrate one of my specialties that was to "Open Your Heart." It's a technique where I guide people through a short meditation and then teach them how to open up their heart chakra, followed by an intuitive reading.

Chuck and I walked into the large room set up with dozens of small tables for the practitioners. There were tables for psychics, mediums, Reiki practitioners, people trained in healing with stones and oils and many more unique healers of one kind or another. We went from table to table looking for a sign with my name on it. After we found it, Chuck helped me set up my material and I sat down.

"You get to see two people with your dinner ticket," I reminded Chuck. "I saw that there is an animal psychic here. Would you go see her? See if Bear comes to her?"

"Sure," he said. Then he headed off and I settled in to receive my first guest client.

About thirty minutes later, Chuck stopped by my table when I was between clients. He said, "I had the reading from the animal psychic."

"Yea? What did she say?"

"Bear did talk to her. The woman told me that Bear said 'I didn't know what was happening, so I was surprised when I was no longer here and I was confused. But now I think I understand.' And she said 'Bear wants you to write something about her. To tell people, to write her story.'" He looked at me warmly.

I cleared my throat and said, "Really, she said that?" I had not told Chuck about the conversation I had with Bear on the trail.

"Yes, she did, Sandy."

Bear couldn't have made herself clearer…

-Eight-

So there it is: the story of my life with Bear. All I need to do is close my eyes and remember Bear lumbering up to each person in a room full of people, sitting beside each person long enough for him or her to bend over and gently pet her, a smile coming to everyone's faces. The light of her love and gentle energy shone around them. She was a gift not only to me, but also to many, many others as well. Yes, she earned her wings.

So I guess that means it's time for Bear to leave the "in between" for good. Her soul will be following Echo through to the glorious light of where all life continues. I don't quite know what or where that is, of course, but I am certain it is a place of All Love, so she clearly belongs there.

Dear my precious sunshine, my sweet Bear,

Bear, you are always in my heart. Go with Echo and be with all the others and send them my love. Thank you for all you did for me and for everyone else who grew to love you too. Until we meet again.

Your momma, soul mate and your admirer,
Sandy

****

The most powerful lesson that Bear taught me on a daily basis was the power of living in "the now:" being present in the moment, free of racing thoughts, regrets, to-do lists and worries. Each time we connected, whether it was through our shared experiences with others, through our hugs, physical touches or just sitting side by side, I was well aware of our limited time together. In that dark "knowing," the greatest gift of love and light arose. We cannot have light without darkness. Bear was my light.

Conclusion

One morning a few months after Bear's death, I headed upstairs to sit and meditate. I turned on soft music and settled back on the soft, comfy chair in my bedroom. Without any particular thoughts on my mind, I closed my eyes. Suddenly, like a flash, a vision came to my mind's eye. I saw Bear in full view. She was once again in the "in between," but this time I could sense that she had just entered it from the light. She stood still in that hazy place. My eyes caught something black weaving through and around her legs. It took me just a second to realize it was Oscar, the cat. My breath caught and my heart filled with joy.

Oscar was a regular volunteer with AEAR for many years. He and his proud parents, George and Liz, attended our pet therapy night at the local nursing home each month. He was quite a celebrity there, wearing his red harness, strutting down the hallways leading one or the other of his parents with confidence. He'd curl up on peoples' beds and sit quietly in others' laps.

Oscar developed cancer about six months ago. His folks used various treatments available in Western and alternative medicine to save him. It was an uphill battle as they ran out of options to treat him. Before I sat down to meditate that morning, I received an e-mail from Liz. Oscar died quietly and peacefully at home in George's arms the day before. I closed the e-mail without responding, choosing instead to wait until I had more time later to send them a respectable sympathy note.

When I closed my eyes to meditate a short time later, Oscar was no longer on my mind. I was focused on quieting my mind. So I was completely taken aback when I saw Oscar, clear as day, weaving in and around Bear's legs.

Then I remembered something Liz had said to me months ago during our monthly pet therapy session. Liz and I stood in the elevator at the nursing home, with other volunteers and pets, going up to the third floor. Bear and Oscar were standing side by side. Liz looked down at Oscar and Bear, "That's the funniest thing," she began, shaking her head, looking down on Oscar and Bear and smiling, "how much Oscar loves Bear. Do you ever notice how he weaves through her legs all the time? He always wants to be with her."

In that elevator I looked down at the two of them and then at Liz, "No, I guess I never noticed because I'm too busy managing all the volunteers and animals and most of the time Bear is with another volunteer and following behind me." Smiling I added, "That's really neat."

Sitting in my chair that gray, overcast morning, a tear fell down my cheek, my chest full of pride and joy. I whispered, "Good girl, Sunshine. You take care of Oscar now. I love you." With a chuckle, I thought, *she's still providing reassurance and her love.* And with that, the two faded away.

I encourage more people to consider adopting a senior pet. The good far outweighs the bad. Love and hugs, SKW

About the Author

Sandy Kamen Wisniewski is the founder and director of Animal Education and Rescue (AEAR) since 2003. She has been a dog trainer since 1993 through her company, Compassionate Dog Training.

In 2014, Sandy started a holistic health and wellness business called, Mindful Spirit. Sandy practices Spiritual Healing, Reiki, Nutritional Therapy, and is certified in Past Life Regression and Tapping. To learn more, please visit www.mindfulspirit.net.

Sandy lives in Libertyville, Illinois with her husband, Chuck, eight-year-old son, Danny, and assortment of rescue animals. She also has two grown children.

Additional books by Sandy:
How to Start Your Own Pet Sitting Service
I Can't Stop Shaking, Over Ten Million People Live with Essential Tremor
The Animal Warrior
To learn more about her books, please visit

www.sandykamenwisniewski.com

All proceeds for this book benefit Animal Education and Rescue, a 501(c)3 humane society. Learn more about Animal Education and Rescue at www.aear.org and follow them on Facebook

Thank you to The Pet Sitters of America, Inc. www.petsittersofamerica.com for being the largest sponsor of Animal Education and Rescue.

Made in United States
North Haven, CT
27 May 2022

19605475R00038